The Employ

All books in the Employment Law Library are sent for free to members of the HR Inner Circle.

Published by Employment Law Services Limited, Unit 3, Chequers Farm, Chequers Lane, Watford, Hertfordshire WD25 0LG

ISBN 978-1-913925-04-8

Employment Status

By Daniel Barnett

Acknowledgments

This is the tenth in my series of small employment law books. They are designed to give HR professionals and those without a formal law degree a solid grounding in a subject that they won't learn about through normal avenues.

I'd like to thank Jennie Hargrove for her help with the content, Tincuta Moscaliuc for the layout and design, Aaron Gaff for proofreading and Maria Rodriguez for converting the book to the formats needed for Amazon.

Finally, I'd like to thank David Appleton for his help with the content of this book.

Daniel Barnett
May 2021

ABOUT THE AUTHOR

Daniel Barnett is a leading employment law barrister practising from Outer Temple Chambers. With 25 years' experience defending public and private sector employers against employment claims, he has represented a Royal Family, several international airlines, FTSE-100 companies and various NHS Trusts and local authorities. Employee clients include David & Victoria Beckham's nanny and Paul Mason (subject of the ITV documentary 'Britain's Fattest Man').

Daniel is a past chair of the Employment Lawyers' Association's publishing committee and electronic services working party. He is the author or co-author of eight books, including the Law Society Handbook on Employment Law (currently in its 8th edition). He is the creator of the Employment Law (UK) mailing list, an email alerter bulletin service sending details of breaking news in employment law three times a week to 30,000 recipients.

Legal directories describe him as 'extremely knowledgeable and [he] can absorb pages of instructions at lightning speed', 'involved in a number of highly contentious matters', 'singled out for his work for large blue-chip companies', 'combination of in-depth legal knowledge, pragmatism, quick response times and approachability', 'inexhaustible', 'tenacious', 'knowledgeable', and 'an excellent advocate'.

He is one of the leading speakers and trainers on the employment law and HR circuit. He has presented seminars for the House of Commons, the BBC, Oxford University, HSBC, Barclays Bank, Ocado, and dozens of other organisations in-house. In 2013, 2014, 2016, and 2019 he designed — and was the sole speaker at — the Employment Law MasterClass national tour.

As well as full-time practice as a barrister and speaker, Daniel is the founder of the HR Inner Circle – a membership club for smart, ambitious HR Professionals. In 2007, he co-founded CPD Webinars Ltd, then the UK's leading webinar training company for lawyers, and sold it to Thomson Reuters in 2011.

Daniel is widely sought after as a commentator in both broadcast and print media on all legal issues. Since 2010 he has presented the Legal Hour on LBC Radio. In 2019, he launched Employment Law Matters, a weekly podcast with short explanations of employment law topics. Subscribe at www.danielbarnett.co.uk/podcast

www.danielbarnett.co.uk
Outer Temple Chambers
Strand, London

DANIEL BARNETT
BARRISTER

SUBSCRIBE

HOME   PLAYLISTS   COMMUNITY   CHANNELS   ABOUT

Try these f

CAN PRESIDENT TRUMP PARDON HIMSELF?
6:57

HELP I'M BEING BULLIED AT WORK
13:45

LBC
7:05

HOW TO HANDLE DISCIPLINARY, DISMISSAL AND PERFORMANCE MANAGEMENT SITUAT
1:53:34

Trump

Help - I'm being bullied at work: a practical guide for...
Daniel Barnett
4.5K views • 3 weeks ago

The most heartbreaking, emotional call I've ever take...
Daniel Barnett
1.2K views • 3 weeks ago

How to Handle Disciplinary, Dismissal and Performance...
Daniel Barnett
688 views • 1 month ago

ASK THE PRESIDENT
EMPLOYMENT TRIBUNALS PRESIDENT (E&W) JUDGE BARRY CLARKE
1:13:52

FAIRNESS IN REDUNDANCY SELECTION
REBECCA TUCK QC
44:01

HELP I'M BEING BULLIED AT WORK
13:45

Ask the President: Judge Barry Clarke, President of...
Daniel Barnett
8K views • 2 weeks ago

Fair Redundancy Dismissals with Rebecca Tuck QC
Daniel Barnett
1K views • 2 weeks ago

Help - I'm being bullied at work: a practical guide for...
Daniel Barnett
4.5K views • 3 weeks ago

EMPLOYMENT LAW MATTERS

CHANGING TERMS AND CONDITIONS AFTER A TUPE TRANSFER

004 Giving References. Can you? Should you?
Employment Law

005 Private Life and Social Media
Employment Law

THE UK'S LEADING
YOUTUBE CHANNEL FOR
LAW EXPLAINER VIDEO

WWW.YOUTUBELEGAL.CO.UK

Contents

All employment and HR practitioners are competing for work in a market where clients are more conscious of spend, and competitors from ABSs & large independent consultancies encroach into the market.

In Intelligent Marketing for Employment Lawyers you will discover how the internet can revolutionise the way you do business and generate new clients, as well as increasing fees and obtaining more work from existing clients.

Visit
GO.DANIELBARNETT.COM/BOOKS
for more information.

Introduction

The world of work has changed significantly over the past 20 years or so, with more and more individuals engaged in what has been dubbed the 'gig economy', where someone may do several different types of work to earn a living. The use of digital platforms to engage services has become commonplace, which in turn has affected the way that people are engaged to deliver those services.

Consumers may not worry about the individual who delivers their pizza or drives them to the airport, but it's a different story for the business engaging the individual to deliver the service, and for the individual themselves. Understanding the status of an individual you are engaging is crucial, as different legal rights and obligations flow from the arrangement, depending on the nature of the particular relationship.

In this book, we will examine the different sorts of relationships that arise in the world of work, how they differ, and how to determine whether someone is an employee, a worker or an independent contractor. We will also look briefly at other types of relationship, such as directors and other officers, employee shareholders, agency workers and volunteers.

Chapter 1
The key types of relationship

In the UK, there are three main types of working relationship that are recognised: the employee, the worker and the independent contractor (also commonly known as a freelancer or self-employed person). Different employment law, tax and immigration regimes apply, depending on which category a person falls into, and it is possible for someone to be treated as an employee for legal purposes and an independent contractor for tax purposes, or vice versa.

The problem for businesses and individuals alike is that the 'rules' on what constitutes an employment relationship are multifaceted, and that they mainly apply in a cumulative manner, meaning that you have to carry out a balancing exercise in each case, putting each of the relevant factors on one side or the other, and then stand back and look at the overall picture, asking: is this person an employee, a worker or an independent contractor? In some cases, the answer is clear, but in others, it's much more finely balanced. See *Hall (Inspector of Taxes) V Lorimer* [1994] 1 All ER 250 for the first case which laid down this approach.

In addition, the label that the parties place on their relationship does not provide the entire answer, as it's the reality of the day-to-day relationship that counts (*Autoclenz Ltd v Belcher* [2011] UKSC 41). Having a beautifully drafted independent contractor's agreement in place will create a presumption that the parties have that arrangement, but it will ultimately make little difference if the individual is, in reality, treated like an employee.

It is interesting that while in most non-employment situations the intentions of contracting parties are usually regarded as primary, when determining the nature of an employment relationship, the courts will not be bound by the declared intentions of the parties, or by the label they apply to their relationship, unless all other factors are evenly balanced (*Dacas v Brook Street Bureau (UK) Ltd* [2004] IRLR 358).

The key differences between an employee, a worker and an independent contractor

In a nutshell, an employee enjoys the full panoply of employment rights contained in the legislation, a worker is entitled to some of them, and an independent contractor is usually only entitled to the rights contained in their contract, with a few exceptions. The Appendix to this book contains a table examining the different rights accorded to the different categories of worker.

However, there are other reasons for establishing the true relationship between two parties. The first is tax, as employees and the self-employed are treated differently by Her Majesty's Revenue and Customs (HMRC). The second reason is that an employer can be vicariously liable for the torts committed by their employees when the wrongful act is done in the course of employment, whereas a self-employed person will generally bear responsibility for their tortious acts themselves.

Another reason is that intellectual property rights in works created by an employee in the course of their employment belong to the employer, whereas a specific agreement to assign such rights would have to be entered into between an independent contractor and the principal for which they create the work.

Finally, immigrants have different entry routes into the UK as employees compared to self-employed people.

Chapter 2:
What is an employee?

An employee is defined in section 230 of the *Employment Rights Act 1996* as:

> "*an individual who has entered into or works under (or, where the employment has ceased, worked under) a contract of employment.*"

A contract of employment is defined as:

> "*a contract of service or apprenticeship, whether express or implied, and (if it is express) whether oral or in writing.*"

A contract of service is not defined, but it is a rather old-fashioned term (harking back to the days of masters and servants) which effectively means a contract of employment. If this feels all rather circular, that's because it is. What is worth noting, though, is that a written contract is not a pre-requisite for someone to be an employee, although there must be a contractual relationship, even if the terms are oral, and/ or implied (*Hewlett Packard Ltd v O'Murphy* [2002] IRLR 4). This is to be contrasted with a volunteer, where there is no contractual relationship between the parties, and the volunteer can just come and go as they please, in theory at least.

A contractual relationship can be implied between two parties from their conduct towards one another, where it is necessary to do so (*James v Greenwich London Borough Council* [2008] EWCA Civ 35). The Court of Appeal cited from an earlier case to explain what was meant by 'necessary':

> " … *necessary [means] to give business reality to a transaction and to create enforceable obligations between parties who are dealing with one another in circumstances in which one would expect that business reality and those enforceable obligations to exist.*"

A contract will not be implied where the court infers that the parties would have behaved in exactly the same way if there had been no contract. A typical scenario is where there has been an agency relationship, with a contract between the worker and the agency, and between the agency and the end user. The worker will sometimes argue that a contract has been implied directly between them and the end user. This has become less likely since the Agency Workers Regulations 2010 came into force.

However, it is desirable to have a comprehensive written contract in place as it will create certainty between the parties. The contract is also the first place that the Employment Tribunal and the courts will look when deciding a person's status, although since *Uber BV and others v Aslam and others* [2021] UKSC 5, tribunals will pay less heed to what the contract says and more heed to what the parties do.

It is important to note that 'employee' can be defined differently for different purposes. For example, in the *Equality Act 2010*, 'employment' is defined in section 83 as follows:

> *"(a) employment under a contract of employment, a contract of apprenticeship or a contract personally to do work;*
>
> *(b) Crown employment;*
>
> *(c) employment as a relevant member of the House of Commons staff; or*
>
> *(d) employment as a relevant member of the House of Lords staff."*

The *Transfer of Undertakings (Protection of Employment) Regulations 2006* (TUPE) have a different definition of an 'employee', namely, "*any individual who works for another person whether under a contract of service or apprenticeship or otherwise but does not include anyone who provides services under a contract for services*".

Under the *Health and Safety at Work etc. Act 1974*, an employee is defined simply as "*an individual who works under a contract of employment*", but expressly includes apprentices, police constables and police cadets.

We will examine how to decide whether someone is an employee in Chapter 5, but let's look first at what statutory rights an employee has.

The employee's rights

There is a long list of statutory rights inherent in being an employee. These are as follows:

- The right not to be unfairly dismissed (subject to a requirement to have been continuously employed for at least two years ending with the effective date of termination, unless the dismissal is for an automatically unfair reason).

- The right to receive a written statement of employment particulars.

- The right to an itemised pay statement.

- The right to receive the National Minimum Wage and National Living Wage.

- The right not to suffer unauthorised deductions from wages.

- The right not to have to make payments to an employer.

- The right to receive statutory sick pay, holiday pay and parental leave pay.

- The right to a guarantee payment (subject to having been continuously employed for at least a month).

- The right of shop and betting workers to opt-out of Sunday working.

- The right not to be dismissed or suffer a detriment in relation to:

  ○ Jury service

  ○ Taking certain actions related to health and safety

  ○ Refusing to do Sunday work as a shop or betting worker

  ○ Their rights under the Working Time Regulations

  ○ Being the trustee of an occupational pension scheme

  ○ Being an employee representative

  ○ Exercising their right to time off work for study or training

  ○ Making a protected disclosure

  ○ Their rights to leave for family and domestic reasons

  ○ Their rights to the receipt of tax credits

- Exercising flexible working rights
- Refusing to be an employee shareholder
- Trade union membership or activities
- The right to take time off work to:
  - Undertake public duties
  - Look for work or arrange training
  - Participate in ante-natal care
  - Accompany a woman participating in ante-natal care
  - Attend adoption appointments
  - Care for a dependent
  - Undertake pension scheme trustee duties
  - Undertake employee representative duties
  - Undertake trade union duties and activities
- The right to make a request for study or training.
- The right to a companion during a disciplinary or grievance hearing.
- The right to be offered alternative work before being suspended on medical grounds.
- The right to be paid during suspension on medical grounds.

- Rights in relation to:
  - Maternity leave
  - Adoption leave
  - Parental leave
  - Shared parental leave
  - Paternity leave
  - Parental bereavement leave
- The right to request flexible working.
- The right to receive statutory minimum notice, dependent on length of continuous employment.
- The right to receive a statutory redundancy payment, dependent on length of continuous employment.
- The right to receive certain payments upon the insolvency of an employer.
- Rights in relation to working time, night work, rest breaks and annual leave.
- The right not to be discriminated against because of:
  - Age
  - Disability
  - Gender reassignment

- Marriage and civil partnership

- Race

- Sex

- Sexual orientation

- The right not to be harassed or victimised.

- The right to have their employment transferred, unchanged, when there is a transfer of an undertaking or business (or part thereof) or where there is a service provision change.

- Health and safety protection.

- Auto-enrolment in a pension scheme.

A comparative table setting out how these rights compare with those of a worker and those of an independent contractor can be seen in Appendix 1.

Chapter 3:
What is a worker?

A worker is defined in section 230 of the *Employment Rights Act 1996* as:

> *"an individual who has entered into or works under (or, where the employment has ceased, worked under)—*
>
> *(a) a contract of employment, or*
>
> *(b) any other contract, whether express or implied and (if it is express) whether oral or in writing, whereby the individual undertakes to do or perform personally any work or services for another party to the contract whose status is not by virtue of the contract that of a client or customer of any profession or business undertaking carried on by the individual."*

The same or a materially similar definition is used in other legislation, such as the *Equality Act 2010*, the *Working Time Regulations 1998* and the *National Minimum Wage Act 1998*. In *Alemi v Mitchell* [2021] IRLR 262, the Employment Appeal Tribunal held that there is no practical difference between the definition of 'worker' under the *Employment Rights Act 1996* and the *Equality Act 2020*, despite slightly different wording.

The definition means that there are three elements to being a worker:

1. the individual has to work under a contract;

2. the individual has to undertake to perform the work personally; and

3. the other party is not a customer or client of the individual under that contract.

These workers are sometimes called 'limb (b) workers' because the precise section of the *Employment Rights Act 1996* in which the definition occurs is section 230(b) (hence, limb 'b').

Section 296(1) of the *Trade Union and Labour Relations (Consolidation) Act 1992* defines workers similarly, as follows:

> *"an individual who works, or normally works or seeks to work—*
>
> *(a) under a contract of employment, or*
>
> *(b) under any other contract whereby he undertakes to do or perform personally any work or services for another party to the contract who is not a professional client of his, or*

> *(c) in employment under or for the purposes of a government department (otherwise than as a member of the naval, military or air forces of the Crown) in so far as such employment does not fall within paragraph (a) or (b) above."*

These definitions mean that the term 'worker' in these statutes includes employees, but can also encompass individuals who do not fall squarely into that category. The key criteria are that a worker agrees to carry out the work personally and that the other party is not a client or customer of the person carrying out the work or services.

The personal service requirement has been the subject of what the Employment Appeal Tribunal has called the 'dominant purpose' test, under which the courts decide whether the dominant purpose of an arrangement was that the person was to provide personal service. If so, and if there was no right to send a substitute, then the person was likely to be a worker. (*James v Redcats (Brands) Ltd* [2007] ICR 1006).

Later cases have established that control is another key component of worker status. In *Jivraj v Haswani* [2011] UKSC 40, the Supreme Court held that an arbitrator was not a worker because he was not under the control of the other party and he could not send a substitute, even though he provided personal services and was paid a fee. The importance of control and personal service was also highlighted by the Court of Appeal in *Halawi v WDFG UK Ltd t/a World Duty Free* [2015] IRLR 50, a case involving a beauty consultant whose services were provided via a limited company and employment agency, and who had a right of substitution. However, in *Bates van Winkelhof v Clyde & Co LLP* [2014] UKSC 32, Baroness Hale cautioned that subordination (control) may be an aid to distinguishing workers from other self-employed people, but it is not a freestanding and universal characteristic of being a worker.

Mutuality of obligations is often absent from a worker relationship, and people have been found to be workers (and indeed employees) who accept jobs on an assignment-by-assignment basis. For example, see *McMeechan v Secretary of State for Employment* [1997] ICR 549; *Cornwall County Council v Prater* [2006] ICR 731 and *James v Redcats (Brands) Ltd* [2007] ICR 1006. However, where an individual only works intermittently or on a casual basis for another person, that may, depending on the facts, tend to indicate a degree of independence which is incompatible with worker status. See *Windle v Secretary of State for Justice* [2016] EWCA Civ 459; [206] ICR 721, para 23.

A useful way of picturing the key differences between a worker and a self-employed person is to envisage someone like a plumber whom you call to fix a leaky pipe. As the customer, typically, you have no say over whether the plumber can send someone else to do the job, and little say over when the plumber turns up or how they do the repair. You don't provide the tools, and you can't stop the plumber from prioritising another customer over you. There is no contract between you and the plumber between jobs, and there's effectively nothing you can do if the plumber calls up to say they've changed their mind and isn't coming (even if you've spent all morning waiting in for them!).

With a worker, once engaged by you, they have to turn up, can't send someone else without your permission and are subject to greater controls by you over when and how they do the work.

The difference between a worker and an employee is often harder to discern. Again, thinking of a typical employee and comparing them with a typical worker can help to highlight the differences. A typical employee has a regular and predictable work pattern and is not engaged on a job-by-job basis. The employee can expect to be given work by the employer and is obliged to do it, whereas a worker has no expectation of being offered work and can turn it down if offered. Typical workers will be freelancers, zero-hours workers and casual staff. It has been suggested that the term 'dependent contractor' is a better term to describe a worker. The Supreme Court's decision in the Uber case (*Uber BV and others v Aslam and others* [2021] UKSC 5), which we examine in detail in Chapter 6, illustrates one type of worker arrangement which is not an employment one.

It is important to note that the concept of a worker only exists in employment law and not in tax law. This means that for tax purposes a worker will either be an employee or a self-employed contractor. The rule of thumb is that a worker (so long as they are not in actuality an employee) is usually treated as a self-employed contractor by HMRC.

We look at the differences between employees, workers and self-employed contractors in more detail in the Appendix to this book.

The worker's rights

The list of statutory rights inherent in being a worker is significantly shorter than that for employees. A worker has the following rights:

- The right to receive a written statement of employment particulars.

- The right to an itemised pay statement.

- The right to receive the National Minimum Wage and National Living Wage.

- The right not to suffer unauthorised deductions from wages.

- The right not to have to make payments to an employer.

- The right to receive statutory holiday pay.

- Rights in relation to working time, night work, rest breaks and annual leave.

- The right not to suffer a detriment in relation to:

  º Their rights under the Working Time Regulations

  º Making a protected disclosure

  º Trade union membership or activities

- The right to a companion during a disciplinary or grievance hearing.

- The right not to be discriminated against because of:

  º Age

  º Disability

  º Gender reassignment

  º Marriage and civil partnership

  º Race

  º Sex

  º Sexual orientation

- The right not to be harassed or victimised.

- Health and safety protections.

- Auto-enrolment in a pension scheme.

In a 2019 Employment Tribunal decision, *Dewhurst and others v (1) Revisecatch Ltd t/a Ecourier; (2) City Sprint (UK) Ltd* (London Central Employment Tribunal, case numbers 2201909, 2201910, 2201911/2018) the Tribunal found that limb (b) workers transfer under the *Transfer of Undertakings (Protection of Employment) Regulations 2006 (TUPE)*. This decision, which has no binding force but can be viewed as 'persuasive', raises all sorts of questions about what rights under TUPE non-employee workers will have, although it does not give non-employee workers a right to unfair dismissal, as the definition of 'employee' in the *Employment Rights Act 1996* does not encompass limb (b) workers.

A comparative table setting out how these rights compare with those of an employee and those of an independent contractor can be seen in Appendix 1.

Chapter 4:
What is an independent contractor?

This is relatively easy to define. It's someone who is in business on their own account and who supplies their work and services to customers and clients. They have no obligation to accept engagements and they have no expectation to be given engagements. They are usually sole traders, although sometimes the term can cover those operating through one-person companies or partnerships.

An independent contractor can become a worker if they agree directly with a client to provide their work or services personally, and become obliged to do the work made available to them.

Whereas an employee works under a 'contract of service', an independent contractor is said to work under a 'contract for services'.

We'll look at the differences between employees, workers and self-employed contractors in more detail in the Appendix to this book.

What are an independent contractor's rights?

- The right to be protected from risks to their health and safety when working in connection with another undertaking.

- The right not to be discriminated against, harassed or victimised where they are employed by a third party.

- In certain circumstances, the right not to suffer a detriment for having made a protected disclosure.

A comparative table setting out how these rights compare with those of an employee and a worker can be seen in Appendix 1.

Chapter 5:

How to determine a person's status

The exercise that the courts and tribunals carry out when they are deciding whether someone is an employee or not entails looking at the terms of any express agreements between the parties, as well as the actual practice on a day-to-day basis. Inferences can be drawn from what parties do. Express and unambiguous terms will tend to prevail, as an express term cannot be overturned by an implied term that contradicts it, but if the parties' invariable practice differs from the express term, then the court may infer that there has been a variation of the term over time, because the parties' intentions have changed over time. Alternatively, the court might decide that the written term does not reflect the reality of the situation, and give preference to the reality.

Many contracts of employment contain a clause that any variations must be in writing, and that may complicate the picture.

Sometimes, parties include a clause in a contract (such as the right for the individual to send a substitute) but do not abide by it in reality. Alternatively, the employer (or its legal adviser) may include such a clause in a contract without meaning it to apply, and where the individual does not understand the intention behind it. These clauses are often referred to as sham clauses. Where the court believes this to be the case, it will then seek to determine what the true relationship is. Assessing the true intentions of the parties is not always helpful as they may well have had different intentions from one another when they entered into the agreement.

Case law has established a number of tests which the courts use to determine the status of an individual. The tests differentiate an employee from an independent contractor. They are usually described as follows:

- The control test

- The economic reality test

- The integration test

The courts will often apply each of these tests to build up a picture of the relationship. However, the tests are not exhaustive, and other factors can be taken into account.

In *Market Investigations Ltd v Minister of Social Security* [1968] 3 All ER 732, the court stated, referring to the question of determining the status of an individual:

"No exhaustive list has been compiled and perhaps no exhaustive list can be compiled of the considerations which are relevant in determining that question, nor can strict rules be laid down as to the relative weight which the various considerations should carry in particular cases."

This observation applies equally as validly now as it did in 1968.

However, there are three criteria which <u>must</u> be satisfied in order for the relationship to be an employment arrangement. These criteria are:

- personal service

- mutual obligation

- control

Personal service

The individual must be contractually obliged to provide their work <u>personally</u> (*Express & Echo Publications Ltd v Tanton* [1999] IRLR 367; *MacFarlane v Glasgow City Council* [2001] IRLR 7).

In *Staffordshire Sentinel Newspapers Ltd v Potter* [2004] IRLR 752, the Employment Appeal Tribunal held that the day-to-day practice of the parties would not be relevant if there was a clear and express contractual term which did not impose obligations on the individual to provide personal service.

Mutual obligation

The employee must be contractually obliged to do work that is given to them to do, and the employer must be obliged to provide work. If there is no obligation to work, then the individual may be a casual worker, a volunteer or an independent contractor but cannot be an employee (*Carmichael v National Power plc* [2000] IRLR 43).

Where there is an express term in the contract stating that there is no mutuality of obligation between the parties, then the contract will not be a contract of employment (*Stevedoring and Haulage Services Ltd v Fuller* [2001] EWCA Civ 651).

This requirement is actually a pre-requisite of a contractual relationship as there could be no contract between parties if they were not mutually obliged to one another. And (to state the obvious) if there is no contract, then there cannot be a contract of employment.

The control test

The 'control' test, which is the oldest test, examines the extent to which the 'employer' controls the work of the individual and derives from the case of *Yewen v Noakes* (1880-81) L.R. 6 Q.B.D. 530. It was expanded upon in *Ready Mixed Concrete (South East) Ltd v Minister of Pensions and National Insurance* [1968] 1 All ER 433. The individual must be contractually obliged to be subject to the control of the person they work for. This means that the employee must ultimately be subject to the directions of the employer. There is no need for a detailed level of control but it must be 'sufficient' within the context of the particular work and the particular business.

The more control the employer has over an individual and their work, the more likely it is that the test will be satisfied. Aspects of that control can include the employer directing:

- when and where the individual carries out the work

- how the individual carries out the work

- that the individual is subject to its rules and disciplinary procedures

- what the individual wears

- what training the individual must have

- how the individual must behave

- what meetings the individual must attend

The results of the control test, like all of the tests, need careful and nuanced analysis, as many employees are not tightly controlled in their work by their managers, either because they are senior, very experienced or very specialised. Conversely, an independent contractor will not usually work completely free of the principal's control and will normally agree with aspects of how the work is to be delivered, such as the price, the timeframe and what is to be done. As with all of the tests, the results will differ on a case-by-case basis.

It is important to understand that a relationship cannot be an employment relationship if one or more of the three requirements of an obligation of personal service, mutuality and sufficient control is absent. However, if all three are present, that does not mean that the relationship will definitely be one of employment. In other words, they are *necessary*, but not necessarily *sufficient* indications to form an employment relationship.

Therefore, the courts have tended to apply other (overlapping) tests as well to enable them to build up an overall picture of the relationship.

The economic reality test

This test (also called the multiple test or the pragmatic test) focuses on details which indicate whether the individual is a person working on their own account. This includes the following factors:

- the amount of financial risk involved for the individual in delivering the work

- whether the individual can profit from performing the work

- what investment, if any, the individual has made in relation to the delivery of the work

- the extent to which the individual has an opportunity to profit from sound management in the performance of the work

- whether the individual recruits their own helpers

- whether the individual provides their own equipment

- whether the hours worked by the individual are fixed by the employer or open-ended

- whether the individual is guaranteed to be paid, and is paid regularly, or whether the individual is paid per job

- whether the person can dictate the terms on which they work, and whether they can work for multiple principals

These factors were first discussed as relevant in *Market Investigations Ltd v Minister of Social Security* [1968] 3 All ER 732 and *Ready Mixed Concrete Ltd v Minister of Pensions* [1968] 2 QB 497.

The factor relating to the opportunity to make a profit was described as the essence of business in a Scottish tax case (*Andrews v King (Inspector of Taxes)* [1991] STC 481. However, profiting from the success of a business does not mean an individual cannot be an employee. See *Secretary of State for Business, Enterprise and Regulatory*

Reform v Neufeld & Howe [2009] EWCA Civ 280, which related to a controlling shareholder.

The way that the individual accounts for tax is part of the picture, but is not decisive given that the employment and tax regimes for these purposes are not identical. The argument can also be circular – it is much more likely to be the case that a person is paid via PAYE, say, because they are regarded as an employee so that the fact of them being paid via PAYE cannot be a decisive indication of an employment status.

The submission of an invoice by the individual, and being registered for VAT will also be relevant but not conclusive. Often, this is a consequence of the label that the 'employer' has insisted upon, rather than a true indicator of the status of the individual.

The integration test

This test, also called the organisation test, looks at how integrated into the business an individual is.

Factors include:

- being subject to the business' rules and disciplinary processes

- having to wear a uniform

- having a right to company sick pay and to holiday pay

- having the right to take parental leave

- enjoying the same benefits as employees

- being allowed access to the intranet
  and other internal systems

One aspect of the test that has been described by the courts is to examine whether the work done by the person is 'ancillary' to the business of the principal. See, for example, *Stevenson, Jordan & Harrison Ltd v MacDonald & Evans* [1952] 1 TLR 101.

For example, in a solicitor's office, lawyers are crucial to the operation of the business whereas cleaners, say, are not. However, this test is not foolproof, as some people whose work is crucial to the business may not be employees. The work of a locum, say, may be crucial to the running of a small law firm if someone goes off sick, but they will usually be a self-employed person or an agency worker. Similarly, the work of the freelance electrician who restores the power after an outage so that the IT system can operate is crucial. Conversely, the work of an employed secretary may be helpful to the business, but not crucial, if every lawyer can do their own typing, answer the phone and so forth.

Summary

There is no single test which can be used to decide a person's status. It's a bit like the 'is it a duck?' test: if it looks like a duck and quacks like a duck, then it's probably a duck. By analogy, if the arrangement looks like employment when you stand back, it probably is. If the picture that emerges is an amalgam of employment and freelancer, then the person will probably be a worker. But these are rules of thumb only.

Chapter 6:
The gig economy –
the leading cases

There have been a number of cases over recent years which have examined the status of individuals working in the gig economy, also known as the 'on-demand' economy. Below, we examine some of these. Whilst each case has to be determined on its own merits, and there are a wide variety of different operating models in the UK gig economy, they are still useful for shining a light on how the courts approach the question of status, and what significance different aspects of an arrangement will have.

A common thread that runs through these cases, and many others, is how businesses will often create documents to convey the impression of an independent contractor whereas the reality shows otherwise. It has been suggested by one commentator[1] that this practice raises the question of whether 'contriving'

----

1   McGaughey, Ewan, Uber, the Taylor Review, Mutuality, and the Duty to Not Misrepresent Employment Status (14 August 2017). (2019) 48(2) Industrial Law Journal 180. Available at SSRN: https://ssrn.com/abstract=3018516

to 'misrepresent' something enables fraud claims, either by staff who seek employment rights, or by public authorities for tax receipts or social security contributions.

A key gig economy case involved Uber, a major and quintessential proponent of the platform-based phenomenon so typical in gig economy cases. This case originated in the Employment Tribunal in 2016, and proceeded through the judicial civil court system until 2021, when the Supreme Court released its judgement. Uber lost in every forum. We examine the Supreme Court's judgement below in some detail as it provides an interesting insight into the approach the courts now take in establishing the status of individuals.

Uber BV and others v Aslam and others [2021] UKSC 5

The working practices examined by the Supreme Court were those that operated in London in 2016. Uber says that it has since changed some of its arrangements with drivers, although it is not clear to what extent the new arrangements would produce a materially different result. Uber's initial reaction at the time of the Supreme Court's judgment in February 2021 was to state that the judgment only applied to a small handful of drivers in the test cases, under 2016 terms and conditions, and not to any other drivers in 2021. However, at the time of writing in April 2021, it has changed its position to state that it intends to ensure all drivers are compensated for arrears of unpaid annual leave and shortfalls in minimum wage.

Uber provides a ride-hailing service (amongst others) which is accessed by users via a mobile app. The drivers (of which there were around 40,000 in the UK in 2016) also access the app to view requests for bookings and are free to choose when they make themselves available to accept them. The drivers use their own cars (whether owned, rented or leased) and must satisfy certain criteria set down by Uber relating to their age, health, car type and so forth. Uber usually sets the fare for each trip, according to a set of variables. The app can be used to allow the passengers to tip the drivers and the drivers and the passengers can rate each other via the app.

The drivers have been treated by Uber in various jurisdictions as self-employed, including in the UK, until a group of London-based drivers brought various claims in the Employment Tribunal, which required them to be 'workers' for the purposes of section 230(3)(b) of the *Employment Rights Act 1996* (ERA), regulation 36(1) of the *Working Time Regulations 1998* (WTR) and section 54(3) of the *National Minimum Wage Act 1998* (NMWA).

The claims in this case were brought against Uber BV, which is a Dutch corporation and parent company of the UK-based Uber companies, and which holds the legal rights to the Uber app. It was also brought against Uber London Limited (ULL), which holds a private hire vehicle (PHV) operator's licence for London and makes provision for the invitation and acceptance of PHV bookings.

The Supreme Court's judgement was concerned with whether, for the purposes of the statutory definition of 'worker', the claimants were to be regarded as working under contracts with ULL whereby they undertook to perform services for ULL, or whether they were performing services for and under contracts with passengers through the agency of ULL.

Essentially, Uber presented itself as a technology provider, with ULL acting as a booking agent for drivers who were approved by ULL to use the app. Uber said that when a ride was booked through the app, a contract was made directly between the driver and the passenger. The fare was calculated by the app and paid by the passengers to Uber BV, which deducted 20 per cent and paid the balance to the driver. Uber characterised this transaction as a service fee charged to the drivers for the provision of the technology and other services.

The Employment Tribunal, the Employment Appeal Tribunal and the Court of Appeal each found that the reality was the drivers were working for Uber as workers. The Supreme Court agreed, and it is that court's judgement that we examine here.

The drivers could work when they wanted and as much or as little as they wanted. They could provide services for other organisations, including direct competitors of Uber. They could choose where to work in the territory covered by their PHV licence, and they were not required to wear any kind of Uber uniform or display any Uber insignia.

The drivers were directed how to behave, however, and statistics were kept on passengers' ratings and comments about drivers, how many trips were cancelled and how many declined when the driver was 'on duty'. Penalties were applied to drivers who cancelled or declined too many trips, and drivers were subjected to a "quality intervention" if their average rating fell below 4.4 over 200 trips or more. A failure to improve would lead to them being removed from the platform and their accounts being deactivated. Deactivation could also result from misconduct.

Where Uber decided to refund a passenger, the fare to the passenger would typically be deducted from the driver's payments, but not always. Sometimes, Uber would pay drivers the cost of cleaning a vehicle soiled by a passenger.

There was no contract between the drivers and ULL but there were written agreements between the drivers and Uber BV, which were inconsistent with the existence of any worker relationship. The 'Services Agreement' setting out the contractual arrangements between Uber BV and the drivers stated that the driver was a 'customer' and that Uber BV agreed to provide electronic services to the driver and the driver agreed to provide transportation services to the passengers.

Under the agreement, the driver agreed that Uber BV did not provide transportation services.

The Services Agreement also stated that Uber BV was the driver's payment collection agent and that payment by a passenger to Uber BV was the same as payment made directly to the driver. The fare was determined by Uber BV as a "recommended amount" which the driver could reduce but not increase. Fares were paid weekly to the driver less the service fee. Uber BV could change the fare calculation at any time and could reduce any fare or cancel it (where a passenger complained).

There were also 'Rider Terms' between the app user (the prospective passenger), Uber BV and ULL. These terms designated ULL as agent for the driver, acting as intermediary between the user and the driver. The Rider Terms granted a licence to the user to use the app.

As there was no contract directly between ULL and the drivers, the nature of their relationship had to be inferred from their conduct. An important feature of the context against which the parties conducted themselves was the legal requirements governing their respective operations in London. ULL was required by law to hold a PHV operator's licence in order to accept bookings, and the drivers needed to hold a PHV driver's licence to drive the passengers making the bookings. The Supreme Court found that there could be no agency arrangement between ULL and the drivers because there was no contract between them whereby the driver authorised ULL to be its agent. The fact that the Rider Terms purported to do so could not be effective because the driver was not a party to the Rider Terms. Furthermore, the contract between Uber BV and the driver did not include ULL, nor did it confer upon the driver authority to accept requests from ULL to accept a trip request.

An agency relationship could have been created by the principal (the driver in this case) conferring authority on the agent (ULL) to act on the driver's behalf, but the driver would have had to have represented to the passenger that ULL was authorised to act as the driver's agent. However, there was no evidence that any driver had ever done that.

So, the Supreme Court concluded that ULL contracted with passengers as principal, and not as agent of the drivers, and that it could not perform its contractual obligations to the passengers nor its regulatory obligations as a licensed operator without employees or sub-contractors to perform the driving services for it. Therefore, ULL had to enter into contracts with drivers.

The Supreme Court also examined the older Supreme Court case of *Autoclenz Ltd v Belcher* [2011] UKSC 41, which had distinguished employment contracts from other sorts of contracts, in that the courts can focus on the reality of the situation where written employment documentation may not reflect the reality of the employment relationship. The justification for this approach was that the employment rights asserted by the claimants were not contractual rights but statutory rights, and the courts had to decide whether the claimants qualified for those rights irrespective of what the contracts stated.

The Court also stated that it was not appropriate to take the contract as the starting point in determining whether an individual fell within the definition of a worker, as the unequal power balance between the individual and the employer meant that the individual had little or no ability to influence the terms that gave rise to the need for statutory protection. In the Uber case, the drivers had no practical possibility of negotiating any different terms to the Services Agreement. In addition, creating contractual terms which excluded the individual from the terms of statutory protections indirectly offended against the prohibition on contracting out contained in the relevant legislation, were of no effect and had to be disregarded.

The Court found five aspects of the Employment Tribunal's findings which it said demonstrated that the transportation service performed by drivers and offered to passengers through the Uber app was very tightly defined and controlled by Uber, and point to the drivers being workers.

First, and of major importance, the remuneration paid to drivers for the work they did was fixed by Uber and the drivers had no say in it (other than by choosing when and how much to work). The notional freedom to charge a passenger less than the fare set by Uber was of no possible benefit to drivers, as any discount offered would come entirely out of the driver's pocket and the delivery of the service was organised so as to prevent a driver from establishing a relationship with a passenger that might generate future custom for the driver personally. Uber also fixed the amount of its own 'service fee' which it deducted from the fares paid to drivers. Uber's control over remuneration further extended to the right to decide in its sole discretion whether to make a full or partial refund of the fare to a passenger in response to a complaint by the passenger about the service provided by the driver.

Second, the contractual terms on which drivers performed their services were dictated by Uber. Not only were drivers required to accept Uber's standard form of written agreement, but the terms on which they transported passengers were also imposed by Uber and drivers had no say in them.

Third, although drivers had the freedom to choose when and where (within the area covered by their PHV licence) to work, once a driver was logged onto the Uber app, a driver's choice about whether to accept requests for rides was constrained by Uber. Unlike taxi drivers, PHV operators and drivers were not under any regulatory obligation to accept such requests. Uber itself retained an absolute discretion to accept or decline any request for a ride. Where a ride was offered to a driver through the Uber app, however, Uber exercised control over the acceptance of the request by the driver in two ways. One was by controlling the information provided to the driver. The fact that the driver, when informed of a request, was told the passenger's average rating (from previous trips) allowed the driver to avoid low-rated passengers who could be problematic. Notably, however, the driver was not informed of the passenger's destination until the passenger was picked up and therefore had no opportunity to decline a booking on the basis that the driver did not wish to travel to that particular destination.

The second form of control was exercised by monitoring the driver's rate of acceptance (and cancellation) of trip requests. A driver whose percentage rate of acceptances fell below a level set by Uber London (or whose cancellation rate exceeded a set level) received an escalating series of warning messages which, if performance did not improve, led to the driver being automatically logged off the Uber app and shut out from logging back on for ten minutes. This measure was described by Uber as a 'penalty'. Uber argued that this practice was justified because refusals or cancellations of trip requests caused delay to passengers in finding a driver and led to customer dissatisfaction. The question, however, was not whether the system of control operated by Uber was in its commercial interests, but whether it placed drivers in a position of subordination to Uber. The Court found that it plainly did.

Fourth, Uber exercised a significant degree of control over the way in which drivers delivered their services. The fact that drivers provided their own car meant that they had more control than most employees would have over the physical equipment used to perform their work. Nevertheless, Uber vetted the types of car that could be used. Moreover, the technology which was integral to the service was wholly-owned and controlled by Uber and was used as a means of exercising control over drivers. Thus, when a ride was accepted, the Uber app directed the driver to the pick-up location and from there to the passenger's destination. Although it was not compulsory for a driver to follow the route indicated by the Uber app, customers could complain if a different route was chosen and the driver bore the financial risk of any deviation from the route indicated by the app which the passenger had not approved.

The Court said that a further potent method of control was the use of the ratings system whereby passengers were asked to rate the driver after each trip and the failure of a driver to maintain a specified average rating resulted in warnings and, ultimately, in termination of the driver's relationship with Uber. Whilst it was commonplace for digital platforms to invite customers to rate products or services, typically, such ratings were merely made available as information which assisted customers in choosing which product or service to buy. The way in which Uber made use of customer ratings was materially different. The ratings were not disclosed to passengers to inform their choice of driver but were used by Uber purely as an internal tool for managing performance, and as a basis for making termination decisions where customer feedback showed that drivers were not meeting the performance levels set by Uber. The Court said that this is a classic form of subordination that is characteristic of employment relationships.

The fifth significant factor was that Uber restricted communication between passenger and driver to the minimum necessary to perform the particular trip and took active steps to prevent drivers from establishing any relationship with a passenger capable of extending beyond an individual ride. When booking a ride, a passenger was not offered a choice among different drivers and their request was simply directed to the nearest driver available. Once a request was accepted, communication between driver and passenger was restricted to information relating to the ride and was channelled through the Uber app in a way that prevented either from learning the other's contact details. Likewise, collection of fares, payment of drivers and handling of complaints were all managed by Uber in a way that was designed to avoid any direct interaction between passenger and driver. A stark instance of this was the generation of an electronic document which, although styled as an 'invoice' from the driver to the passenger, was never sent to the passenger and, though available to the driver, recorded only the passenger's first name and not any further details. Further, drivers were specifically prohibited by Uber from exchanging contact details with a passenger or contacting a passenger after the trip ended other than to return lost property.

The Court went on to find that the Employment Tribunal was entitled to find that time spent by the claimants working for Uber was not limited (as Uber argued) to periods when they were actually driving passengers to their destinations, but included any period when the driver was logged into the Uber app within the territory in which the driver was licensed to operate and was ready and willing to accept trips.

Pimlico Plumbers Ltd v Smith

The Supreme Court examined the issue of employment status in a different model in the case of *Pimlico Plumbers Ltd & another (Appellants) v Smith (Respondent)* [2018] UKSC 29.

Between August 2005 and April 2011, Mr Smith, a plumbing and heating engineer, did work for Pimlico, a company that conducts a substantial plumbing business in London. In August 2011, Mr Smith issued proceedings against Pimlico and its owner in the Employment Tribunal. Mr Smith alleged that he had been an employee, and had been unfairly dismissed.

He also claimed that he had been a worker and that he had suffered unlawful deductions from his wages, had not been paid for a period of his statutory annual leave and had been discriminated against by reference to a disability.

The Tribunal found that Mr Smith was not an employee, but also found that Mr Smith had been a 'worker' for Pimlico within the meaning of section 230(3) of the *Employment Rights Act 1996*, a 'worker' for Pimlico within the meaning of regulation 2(1) of the *Working Time Regulations 1998*, and that he had been in Pimlico's 'employment' within the meaning of section 83(2)(a) of the *Equality Act 2010*.

Appeals against these findings brought by Pimlico to the Employment Appeal Tribunal and the Court of Appeal failed.

The Supreme Court referred to the contractual documents having been "carefully choreographed" to serve inconsistent objectives; on the one hand, to present the operatives to the public as part of its workforce and on the other to render the operatives self-employed in business on their own account. A third identified objective was to enable Pimlico to exert a substantial measure of control over its operatives.

Mr Smith's contracts with Pimlico, including the company's manual, gave him no express right to appoint a substitute to do his work, although he could bring an assistant, which did not amount to substitution, according to the Supreme Court. Mr Smith did also have a limited facility to substitute in circumstances where, if he had quoted for work but another more lucrative job had subsequently arisen, he would be allowed to arrange for the work to be done by another Pimlico operative. The Supreme Court said that it was helpful to assess the significance of Mr Smith's right to substitute another Pimlico operative by reference to whether the dominant feature of the contract remained personal performance on his part.

In coming to the conclusion that Mr Smith was a worker, the Supreme Court noted that the terms of Pimlico's contract with Mr Smith focused on personal performance. The terms referred to "your skills", to a warranty that "you will be competent to perform the work which you agree to carry out" and to a requirement of "a high standard of conduct and appearance". The terms of the accompanying manual included requirements that "your appearance must be clean and smart", that the Pimlico uniform should be "clean and worn at all times" and that "[y]our [Pimlico] ID card must be carried when working for the Company".

To the extent that Mr Smith's facility to appoint a substitute was the product of a contractual right, the limitation of it was significant: the substitute had to come from the ranks of Pimlico operatives, in other words, from those bound to Pimlico by an identical suite of heavy obligations. It was the converse of a situation in which the other party is uninterested in the identity of the substitute, provided only that the work gets done.

The Supreme Court then considered whether the status of Pimlico by virtue of the contract was that of a client or customer of Mr Smith. First, the Supreme Court agreed with the Tribunal's finding that there was an umbrella contract between Mr Smith and Pimlico (that is, a contract which cast obligations on Mr Smith during the periods between his work on assignments for Pimlico).

The Court agreed that there were features of the contract which strongly militated against recognition of Pimlico as a client or customer of Mr Smith. Its tight control over him was reflected in its requirements that he should wear the branded Pimlico uniform; drive its branded van, to which Pimlico applied a tracker; carry its identity card; and closely follow the administrative instructions of its control room.

In addition, the company imposed severe terms as to when and how much it was obliged to pay Mr Smith, which were inconsistent with Mr Smith being a truly independent contractor. The contract made references to "wages", "gross misconduct" and "dismissal" and there was a suite of covenants restrictive of his working activities following termination.

In conclusion, the Court agreed with the Employment Tribunal's finding that Mr Smith was a limb (b) worker. It is to be noted that Mr Smith was also a self-employed person for tax purposes, and that illustrates the fact that tax law does not ecognize 'worker' as a separate category.

Dewhurst and others v (1) Revisecatch Ltd t/a Ecourier; (2) City Sprint (UK) Ltd ET/2202512/2016

This was an employment tribunal case which examined the status of couriers.

To become a courier, applicants had to pass a two-day recruitment process. Successful applicants were presented with a document called a 'confirmation of tender to supply courier services', which treated them as self-employed contractors. They had to acknowledge a number of key terms, which included statements that:

- the courier was not under any obligation to provide services

- the company was under no obligation to provide work

- the courier could use a substitute to provide the courier service provided the substitute satisfied certain criteria

- if the courier did not work, they would not get paid

There was no entitlement to holiday, maternity or sick pay and couriers were paid by the job. The couriers did not have to submit invoices and City Sprint automatically calculated the payment due and paid them weekly in arrears (even though City Sprint referred to the process as a "self-billing and invoice system").

Despite the statements in the 'confirmation of tender to supply courier services' document, in reality, couriers:

- had to log into the company's city tracker system when on circuit and log out at the end of the day

- had to wear a company uniform

- had to work when they said they would

- were directed by radio and mobile phone

- were told to smile

The Tribunal held that Ms Dewhurst had been recruited by City Sprint, was integrated into its business and so was a worker during the period she was logged into the City Sprint tracker system.

R (on the application of the Independent Workers Union of Great Britain) v Central Arbitration Committee and Roofoods Ltd t/a Deliveroo [2018] EWHC 3342 (Admin)

This is a decision that has gone against the grain of finding that individuals working in the gig economy were workers.

Deliveroo is an online food delivery company founded in 2013 in London. Deliveroo deliveries are made by bicycle and motorbike riders. The Independent Workers Union of Great Britain (IWGB) applied to the Central Arbitration Committee (CAC) for collective bargaining rights in respect of Deliveroo riders. To be a member of a union, members have to be workers as defined in section 296 of the *Trade Union and Labour Relations (Consolidation) Act 1992*. The CAC declared that Deliveroo riders had a genuine right to use a substitute to perform deliveries, which was inherently incompatible with an obligation to provide personal service. Therefore, Deliveroo riders are not workers. The IWGB applied for judicial review of that decision.

The IWGB's argument was that the definition of 'worker' in section 296 of the *Trade Union and Labour Relations (Consolidation) Act 1992*, and the obligation of personal performance, should be interpreted in a way that does not exclude riders from exercising their rights under Article 11 of the European Convention on Human Rights. This holds that:

> *"Everyone has the right to freedom of peaceful assembly and to freedom of association with others, including the right to form and to join trade unions for the protection of his interests.*

> *No restrictions shall be placed on the exercise of these rights other than such as are prescribed by law and are necessary in a democratic society in the*

interests of national security or public safety, for the prevention of disorder or crime, for the protection of health or morals or for the protection of the rights and freedoms of others."

The High Court rejected the application for judicial review. First, it found that Article 11 was not engaged, as the riders had not been in an employment relationship with Deliveroo for the purposes of domestic or EU law. It said that, even if Article 11 had been engaged, the interference with the riders' rights would have been justified in light of the fact that restrictions are permitted where they are "necessary in a democratic society … for the protection of the rights and freedoms of others". In this case, the restriction was rationally connected to the objective of preserving freedom of business and contract, by limiting the cases in which the burden of collective bargaining should apply.

The High Court also stated that the definition of 'worker' achieved a fair balance between the parties' competing interests. The interference with the riders' rights was limited, as the riders were not prevented from joining unions or making voluntary arrangements, but merely stopped from making use of the legislative mechanism for compulsory union recognition. The three matters for which compulsory collective bargaining could be enforced were pay, hours and holiday. However, hours and holiday were of no real significance where there was no obligation to work personally, and discussion of pay was limited by the absence of such an obligation.

The Court said that the key question was whether the contract under which the individual normally worked contained a personal work obligation, which it did not in this case.

Finally, the Court also rejected the argument that it could adopt a "dominant feature" test following the Supreme Court's judgment in *Pimlico Plumbers*. *Pimlico Plumbers* made clear that the sole test is personal obligation, which could not be usurped by the dominant feature test.

Chapter 7:

The Taylor Review of Modern Working Practices

The *Taylor Review of Modern Working Practices*, released in 2017, reviewed the various ways of working in the UK and considered a range of issues, including the implications of new forms of work; the rise of digital platforms; and the impact of new working models on employee and worker rights, responsibilities, freedoms and obligations. It made 53 recommendations and proposed "seven steps towards fair and decent work with realistic scope for development and fulfilment". These steps contained various 'sub-steps' and included:

1. A fair balance of rights and responsibilities, with everyone having a baseline of protection and routes to enable progression at work.

2. Making taxation of labour more consistent across employment forms, and improving the rights and entitlements of self-employed people.

3. Renaming 'workers' as 'dependent contractors'.

4. Making the distinction between dependent contractors and the genuinely self-employed clearer.

5. The need for additional protections to be provided for dependent contractors with incentives for firms to treat them fairly.

6. All workers being engaged and heard.

7. The need for a more proactive approach to be taken to workplace health.

8. The need for steps to be taken to ensure that people are not stuck at the living wage minimum or face insecurity, but can progress in their current and future work.

The government accepted most of the recommendations of the Taylor Review (see *Good Work – A response to the Taylor Review of Modern Working Practices*, published in February 2018), and a number of legislative changes were made as a result, extending the rights of workers and agency workers. These were the 'quick fix' changes that could be implemented somewhat easily. Other more complex matters needed to be reviewed by government, and the Employment Bill – announced in the Queen's Speech in December 2019 and expected to be published later in 2021 – is expected to address several of the recommendations which have not already been implemented. These recommendations include the right for all workers to request a more predictable and stable contract after 26 weeks' service and the introduction of a single labour market enforcement body to ensure that vulnerable workers are better informed of their rights, and to support businesses in compliance.

Chapter 8:
Agency workers

Agency workers have specific protections conferred by the *Agency Worker Regulations 2010*. Agency workers are individuals who have a contract with a temporary work agency but work temporarily for a third-party hirer. A key aspect of being an agency worker is that the individual agrees to perform work personally, either under a contract of employment or another kind of contract.

An individual is not an agency worker if the agency, or the hirer, is a client or customer of a profession or business undertaking carried on by the individual.

A 'temporary work agency' is a person or entity which either supplies individuals to work temporarily for and under the supervision and direction of hirers or which pays for, receives or forwards payment for the services of individuals who are supplied to work temporarily for and under the supervision and direction of hirers.

A person is not a temporary work agency if they pay for, receive or forward payments for the services of individuals regardless of whether the individuals are supplied to work for hirers.

Therefore, the Regulations apply to temps, including those looking for work through modelling and entertainment agencies, but not people who are found permanent or fixed-term employment by a recruitment agency.

Before looking for work for someone, the agency must give them:

- a key information document

- written terms of engagement - often known as a contract

The key information document is a short explanation of how the person will be paid and what deductions will be applied. It must include:

- the minimum rate of pay the worker can expect

- a sample pay slip giving an estimate of the take home pay after deductions (such as National Insurance, income tax or private healthcare)

- the identity of the payer

- whether any fees need to be paid

- any entitlements to benefits

An agency cannot charge a fee for seeking or finding work for someone, but can charge a fee for extra services, such as CV writing or training.

The written terms of engagement should include:

- whether the worker is employed under a contract for services or a contract of employment

- the notice period

- the pay

- the holiday entitlement

An agency cannot change terms and conditions without consulting first. If agreement is reached, a new document must be issued with the full details of the changes and the date they changed.

Once the agency has found work for the individual, it must issue a written statement that advises the individual of:

- the start date

- how long the contract is likely to last

- the type of work

- any expenses the individual may have to pay

- the location of the work

- their hours of work

- any health and safety risks

- any experience, training or qualifications needed for the role

From the first day of work, an agency worker is entitled to all of the same rights as a worker, including the National Minimum Wage for all work done, whether or not it is recorded on a timesheet. Agency workers also have the same rights as permanent colleagues to use any shared facilities and services provided by their employer, for example:

- a canteen or food and drinks machines

- a workplace creche or mother and baby room

- car parking or transport services, like a local pick-up service or transport between sites

After 12 continuous calendar weeks of employment during one or more assignments, an agency worker qualifies for the same basic working and employment conditions as they would be entitled to for doing the same job if they had been recruited by the hirer directly, either as an employee or a worker. This is known as a regulation 5 right or 'equal treatment'. These rights used not to apply if the agency employed the agency worker directly, an exception called the 'Swedish Derogation', but the exception was removed by the government following the publication of the Taylor Review (see Chapter 7) and so it has not applied since 6 April 2020.

In working out what basic working and employment conditions workers would have been entitled to, it is necessary to look at what a comparable employee's terms and conditions are.

An employee is a comparable employee in relation to an agency worker where both are:

- working for and under the supervision and direction of the hirer

- engaged in the same or broadly similar work having regard, where relevant, to whether they have a similar level of qualification and skills

- the employee works or is based at the same establishment as the agency worker or, where there is no comparable employee working or based at that establishment who satisfies the above requirements, works or is based at a different establishment and satisfies those requirements

These basic rights include:

- pay

- the duration of working time

- night work

- rest periods

- rest breaks

- annual leave

When working out whether the agency worker has completed 12 weeks of continuous employment, some periods of leave are not counted, but pause the calculation. These are when the worker:

- takes a break of six weeks or less

- is on leave due to sickness or injury for up to 28 weeks

- takes annual leave they are entitled to

- does not work because the workplace closes, for example for Christmas or industrial action

- is on jury service for up to 28 weeks

The calculation of the 12-week period does not pause if the agency worker is on leave for:

- pregnancy and up to 26 weeks after childbirth

- adoption leave

- paternity leave

The calculation of the 12-week period has to start again if the agency worker:

- gets a new job at a different workplace

- has a break of more than six weeks between jobs at the same workplace

- stays at the workplace but takes a new role that is 'substantively different'

A substantively different role is one that involves completely new, different work. It could be a combination of differences including:

- skills, or requiring new training

- pay rate

- location

- working hours

An agency worker who considers that the hirer or a temporary work agency has treated them in a manner which infringes a right to the same basic working and employment conditions as a comparable employee may make a written request to the temporary work agency for a written statement containing information relating to the treatment in question.

An agency worker has the right not to suffer a detriment and the right not to be unfairly dismissed (if they are an employee) on the grounds that the agency worker has or is believed by the hirer or the temporary agency to have:

- brought proceedings under the Agency Worker Regulations 2010

- given evidence or information in connection with such proceedings brought by any agency worker

- made a request for a written statement

- done anything under the Regulations in relation to a temporary work agency, hirer, or any other person

- alleged that a temporary work agency or hirer has breached the Regulations

- refused (or proposed to refuse) to forgo a right conferred by the Regulations

It is unlawful to discriminate against an agency worker on the grounds that they:

- are pregnant

- have given birth in the last six months

- are breastfeeding

Discrimination will include:

- the agency refusing to place the agency worker in a job

- the hirer refusing to hire the agency worker

- the job being terminated because the agency worker is pregnant

- the agency refusing to keep the agency worker on its books

- the agency offering only short jobs and giving longer jobs to other agency workers

- the hirer not allowing the agency worker to return after having leave due to maternity

Chapter 9:
Other types of employment relationships

Volunteers

Volunteers often play an important role in charitable organisations. A volunteer will not have the status of an employee or worker because the basic elements of a contractual agreement are not present. A volunteer does not have an expectation to be paid for the work they do and does not receive any pay for it. A volunteer may receive reimbursement of their out-of-pocket expenses though.

A volunteer will still be covered by health and safety law and data protection law.

When does a volunteer become an employee?

Here are some ways of ensuring that a volunteer does not actually have employee status:

- If a volunteer contract is in place, it should avoid prescriptive language such as, "you will be required…", and should instead use phrases such as "we would like you to…" or "it would be helpful for you to...". Obviously, an express statement stating that no employment relations are intended by either party must be included.

- Volunteers must be able to decide when they will work and whether to accept work at all. They will not be subject to the same degree of control as employees, and they should be allowed to choose how to spend their time, if possible, rather than requiring them to carry out specified tasks within set timescales.

- No payment for services should ever be made to volunteers. Only reimbursement for expenses should be paid by reference to valid receipts so as to show how much has been paid and why. Similarly, perks which could be seen as a substitute for payment should be avoided.

In the case of Migrant Advisory Service v Chaudri UKEAT/1400/97 the Employment Appeal Tribunal found that Ms Chaudri was an employee rather than a volunteer. Ms Chaudri started volunteering in 1994, as part of her training. After that, she started to go in on a regular basis, until she was dismissed on 12 September 1996. *The Employment Appeal Tribunal found that she had been* employed as an administrative assistant for 12 hours a week on Mondays, Tuesdays, Wednesdays and Thursdays, from 10 am until 1pm. She was first paid £25 a week, and her pay then increased from £25 to £40 a week. The Migrant Advisory Service (MAS) called these flat-rate payments "voluntary expenses" and no tax or National Insurance contributions were deducted from them.

Ms Chaudri actually incurred no out-of-pocket expenses in attending the MAS. On the basis of the regularity of the days and hours worked, and the payment of what was found to be a salary, the Employment Appeal Tribunal held that the Employment Tribunal was correct to find that Ms Chaudri had been an employee and not a volunteer.

Employee shareholders

The role of employee shareholder was an innovation brought into force in 2013 to give employees more of a stake in a company and to encourage them to help the company do well. In exchange for the company giving the starter at least £2,000 worth of shares, the starter surrendered certain employment rights, most importantly the right to claim unfair dismissal and the right to a statutory redundancy payment. Legal advice was required before the agreement could take effect.

In practice, very few people took up employee shareholder status, and the tax reliefs associated with employee shareholder status ceased to be available for shares acquired on or after 1 December 2016. Although still on the statute books, this status is no longer of any practical interest, although those who became employee shareholders between 2013 and 2016 retain that status.

Directors

Company directors (sometimes called board directors) make the strategic and operational decisions of the company and are responsible for ensuring that the company meets its statutory obligations.

A company director is first and foremost an officeholder, and being appointed a director does not automatically make an individual an employee. However, most executive directors will also be employed under a contract of employment.

It will be the board which will decide whether to grant service contracts to directors, subject to their powers set out in the company's articles. A fixed-term contract with a guaranteed term of more than two years must be first approved by resolution of the members of the company (see section 188 of the *Companies Act 2006*). If it is not, then the provision guaranteeing a term of more than two years is void, to the extent of the contravention, and the contract is deemed to contain a term entitling the company to terminate it at any time by the giving of reasonable notice.

Both the Model Articles and Table A contain provisions relating to the terms upon which a director may be employed. All limited companies must have articles of association, which set the rules company officers must follow when running their companies. Model Articles of Association are the standard default articles a company can use, prescribed by the *Companies Act*

2006. The latest model articles apply by default to all private and public limited companies incorporated on or after 28 April 2013. Table A is the name given to the prescribed format for articles of association of a company limited by shares under the *Companies Act 1985* and earlier legislation.

Directors owe seven key statutory duties to the company they are a director of (which can obviously be supplemented by additional duties provided under a contract of employment). The seven statutory duties of a director are that they must:

- act within their powers under the company's constitution

- promote the success of the company

- exercise independent judgement

- exercise reasonable skill, care and diligence in their role

- avoid or manage conflicts of interest which may affect their objectivity

- not accept benefits from third parties

- declare interests in proposed or existing transactions or arrangements with the company

Breaches of these duties can result in action being taken against the director by the company (through the board), a liquidator (if the company is in liquidation) or the shareholders in certain circumstances.

Directors owe a number of other duties, such as those relating to the preparation, content, circulation and filing of the company's annual reports and accounts, and those under other legislation such as the *Health and Safety at Work Act 2015*, anti-corruption legislation and environmental legislation. Common law duties are also often implied, such as the duty of confidentiality and fiduciary duties. A fiduciary is a person to whom power or property is entrusted for the benefit of someone else. In the context of a company director, fiduciary duties include a duty of confidentiality, a duty of no conflict, and a duty not to profit from their position. Public criticism of the board and the sharing of sensitive corporate information has been found to be a breach of a director's fiduciary duties in a recent High Court case (*Stobart Group Limited v Tinkler* [2019] EWHC 258).

Directors may be indemnified against many risks inherent in their office by way of directors and officers (D&O) insurance, although it is not possible to be indemnified against the unsuccessful defence of or fines imposed in criminal proceedings and penalties imposed by regulatory bodies.

Chapter 10:
Taxation

A detailed examination of the tax regimes applying to employees and the self-employed is beyond the scope of this book, but it is worth examining the key differences.

Employees

The earnings of employees have to be accounted for in their employers' payroll system via the Pay As You Earn (PAYE) system, which enables income tax and National Insurance contributions (NICs) to be collected. Employers have to register with PAYE unless none of the employees are paid £120 or more a week, get expenses and benefits, have another job or receive a pension.

Deductions for income tax and NICs are made from salary or wages, and other income such as tips or bonuses, statutory sick pay and maternity pay. The rate of the tax paid depends on the expected level of earnings within the tax year, with different rates applying to different bands of income. The rate is reflected in the employee's tax code.

Employers who run their own payroll systems have to report to HMRC all payments and deductions on or before each payday by sending a full payment submission (FPS). Annual reports also have to be made on or before the employees' last payday of the tax year (which ends on 5 April). This is done by sending a final FPS. In addition, each employee should be given a P60. Expenses and benefits paid to an employee also have to be reported each year by 6 July by submitting a P11D form.

Workers and the self-employed

Limb (b) workers are treated the same as self-employed contractors from a tax point of view, and have to account to HMRC for their own tax and NI payments. They can offset trading losses and expenses against their income. HMRC are alive to what they call disguised remuneration schemes, however, and have put in place regimes to defeat what they regard as tax evasion schemes. One such is the IR35 regime.

The IR35 regime

This refers to the anti-tax avoidance regime operated by HMRC under which individuals working on a putative freelance basis through a personal service company (PSC), or other intermediary structures, are taxed as if they were an employee of the client where HMRC believe that they would have been taxed in that way if they had been working for the client directly. Clients in this case are also known as 'hirers', 'engagers' or 'end clients'. The individuals are often called "disguised employees". The system of using a PSC is also known as "off-payroll working".

Until April 2021, the intermediaries had primary responsibility for determining the true tax status of the individual working for a private sector client. However, from 6 April 2021, the legal responsibility for determining the status of a contractor performing services will transfer from the intermediary to the private sector client engaging the contractor (this regime already applies to public sector clients). The private sector client will have the primary legal obligation of assessing the contract in advance and determining the IR35 status of the contract.

The rules will only apply to 'medium or large enterprises', which is one which satisfies two or all of the following requirements in the year in question (these figures are for 2020/21):

1. It has a turnover of more than £10.2 million

2. It has a balance sheet total of more than £5.1 million

3. It has more than 50 employees

Non-corporate enterprises will be defined as medium or large by reference to their turnover alone.

From 6 April 2021, each contract will have to be assessed by all medium and large enterprises (and public enterprises, as currently) to determine whether it should be characterised as an employment or self-employment arrangement. This assessment is done via a 'status determination statement' (SDS).

Determining the status of the individual will be done using the same kinds of tests discussed in this book, although there is a tool available on the HMRC website called the 'CEST Test' (Check Employment Status for Tax). The CEST has been criticised by some experts as being too blunt an instrument, and for favouring an outcome which results in an assessment of the individual as an employee.

The assessment must be done with reasonable care; otherwise, the client's obligation to issue an SDS will not have been satisfied. The client must pass the SDS, with reasons for their conclusion, to their contracting party and the individual. Each party must pass the SDS and the reasons for the decision to the next party in the chain, until it reaches the party who or which will pay the fee.

Both the fee payer and the worker can challenge the SDS, and the client then has 45 days within which to decide whether to change the SDS or not. If not, it must give reasons.

Appendix

Right	Employee	Worker	Independent Contractor
Unfair dismissal	Yes	No	No
Written statement of particulars	Yes	Yes	No
Itemized pay statement	Yes	Yes	No
National minimum/living wage	Yes	Yes	No
Unauthorised deductions	Yes	Yes	No
No obligation to pay employer	Yes	Yes	No
Statutory sick, holiday and parental leave pay	Yes	Holiday Pay	No
Guarantee payment	Yes	No	No
Opt out of Sunday working	Yes	No	No
No dismissal or detriment (DDs) re jury service	Yes	No	No
No DDs re health and safety actions	Yes	No	No
No DDs re refusing Sunday work	Yes	No	No
No DDs re asserting rights under the Working Time Regulations	Yes	Yes	No
No DDs re being a trustee of an occupational pension scheme	Yes	No	No
No DDs re being an employee representative	Yes	No	No
No DDs re exercising right to time off work for study or training	Yes	No	No

Key: DD = Detriment or dismissal

Right	Employee	Worker	Independent Contractor
No DDs re making a protected disclosure	Yes	Yes	No
No DDs for exercising leave for family and domestic reasons	Yes	No	No
No DDs for exercising rights to family credits	Yes	No	No
No DDs for exercising flexible working rights	Yes	No	No
Refusing to be an employee shareholder	Yes	No	No
No DDs for trade union membership or activities	Yes	Yes	No
Right to time off (T/O) to undertake public duties	Yes	No	No
T/O to seek work or arrange training	Yes	No	No
T/O to participate in ante-natal care	Yes	No	No
T/O to accompany a woman participating in ante-natal care	Yes	No	No
T/O to attend adoption appointments	Yes	No	No
T/O for caring for a dependent	Yes	No	No
T/O to undertake pension scheme trustee duties	Yes	No	No
T/O to undertake employee representative duties	Yes	No	No
T/O to undertake trade union duties and activities	Yes	No	No
Request for study or training	Yes	No	No
Companion during disciplinary and grievance hearings	Yes	Yes	No
To be offered alternative work before being suspended on medical grounds	Yes	No	No

Key: DD = Detriment or dismissal

90

Right	Employee	Worker	Independent Contractor
To be paid during suspension on medical grounds	Yes	No	No
Maternity leave	Yes	No	No
Adoption leave	Yes	No	No
Parental leave	Yes	No	No
Shared parental leave	Yes	No	No
Paternity leave	Yes	No	No
Parental bereavement leave	Yes	No	No
Request flexible working	Yes	No	No
Receive statutory minimum notice	Yes	No	No
Statutory redundancy payment	Yes	No	No
Payments on insolvency of employer	Yes	No	No
Working time rights	Yes	Yes	No
Rest breaks and annual leave	Yes	Yes	No
Protection from discrimination because of age, disability, gender reassignment, marriage and civil partnership, race, sex, sexual orientation	Yes	Yes	No
Not to be harassed or victimized	Yes	Yes	No
TUPE rights	Yes	Possibly	No
Health and safety	Yes	Yes	No
Auto-enrolment in a pension scheme	Yes	Yes	No

Key: DD = Detriment or dismissal

Also by
Daniel Barnett

Available on Amazon
or visit
go.danielbarnett.com/books

JOIN DANIEL EVERY SATURDAY EVENING AT
9PM WHEN HE PRESENTS THE ALL-NEW

LBC LEGAL HOUR

— OR CATCH UP VIA THE GLOBAL PLAYER,
AT bit.ly/lbclegalhour

SATURDAYS, 9PM

I have updated my 20 Employment Law Policies for small businesses.

If you are an HR professional, they are perfect for incorporating into a staff handbook. If you are a solicitor, they come with a licence for you to resell them or give them away for free to clients.

WWW.POLICIES2020.COM

HR INNER CIRCLE

"The HR Inner Circle has improved my life amazingly, mainly because it means I have to spend less time researching and more time and more time actually doing the work I'm paid for."

Sue Whittle, Employment & Safety Advice LTD

Join to gain access to the monthly HR Inner Circular magazine

jam-packed with amazing information for ambitious HR professionals

What do you get?

1 Monthly live online 'Ask Me Anything' sessions: each month, we host an online video webinar, when you can share your HR problems and ask Daniel anything about employment law. You'll also receive a recording and a transcript each month, so you have a permanent record of the session even if you cannot be there.

—DANIEL BARNETT'S—
(HR) INNER CIRCLE

Please ask your questions now:
1. click 'Raise Hand'; or,
2. type it into the Questions box

"Daniel Barnett is an inspirational, walking and talking 'how to understand mind-boggling employment law handbook!"

Ellie King, HR Manager, RWE Technology

2 A specially recorded audio seminar every month, with HR shortcuts and workarounds you can't get anywhere else.

WWW.HRINNERCIRCLE.CO.UK

3 The monthly Inner Circular magazine, jam-packed with valuable information for ambitious HR professionals.

4 Access to Daniel's exclusive, private, invitation-only online Inner Circle group, where you get to discuss HR problems with other smart, ambitious professionals and download precedents and policies they have shared.

"It's the support and help that you get, the reassurance that you're talking to people who know what they're talking about rather than people just randomly giving information."

Nicky Jolley, HR2DAY LTD

5 Access to the exclusive HR Inner Circle website which includes a back-catalogue of all the HRIC resources since the launch in 2015.

WWW.HRINNERCIRCLE.CO.UK

"This is one of the best investments in yourself and your career you will ever decide to take."

100%
Risk-Free
Guarantee

Only **£86 + VAT**
per month

No long-term contracts.
No notice periods.
No fuss.

Join today!

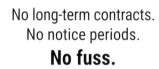

If you are looking for a forum to discuss confidential issues that need prompt employment law advice, then the HR Inner Circle is definitely for you. In addition it offers other tools to help and support. The Facebook group is full of information and solutions to scenarios — invaluable for HR professionals.

- **Sheena Doyle**, Managing Director, The Really Useful HR Company Ltd

It's a forum where you're not afraid to ask stupid questions, even though I'm not usually afraid of doing that. The sheer variety of experience and skillsets ensures there is always an informed discussion. JOIN NOW!!

- **Jon Dews**, HR & Business Partner, Majestic 12 Ltd

If you are looking for a steady stream of thorough, pragmatic, and easily-digestible employment law advice, the HR Inner Circle is a great place to be.

- **Susi O'Brien**, Senior Manager HR, The Action Group

The regular updates are invaluable to not only me, but also my team. We find that they are presented in an easy to digest format and aren't too 'legalistic'.

- **Donna Negus**, Sekoya Specialist Employment Services

WWW.HRINNERCIRCLE.CO.UK

There aren't many other employment law advice services where you get direct access to an employment law barrister at a realistic price. Join the HR Inner Circle now – you won't regret it.

- **Kirsten Cluer**, Owner of Cluer HR, HR Consultancy

I like being able to use the HR Inner Circle Facebook group to ask other members for a second opinion, or for ideas when I get stuck with solving a tricky situation. There's usually someone who has come across the situation before.

- **Helen Astill**, Managing Director, Cherington HR Ltd

When I transitioned from big employers to an SME, I didn't realise how much I would miss having peers to kick ideas around. If you haven't got an internal network, you've got to build an external one. I got so much out of the discussion at an Inner Circle meetup recently and I look forward to getting the Inner Circular.

- **Elizabeth Divver**, Group HR Director, The Big Issue Group

Sign now! The monthly Q & A sessions are invaluable, the magazine is packed full of helpful info, you get lots of goodies and the Facebook page is really informative and a useful sounding board.

- **Caroline Hitchen**, Consultant, Caroline Neal Employment Law

WWW.HRINNERCIRCLE.CO.UK

Being a member of HR Inner Circle is one of the best sources of HR information and advice, and receiving the monthly audio seminars and magazines is extremely helpful and interesting. I can't recommend becoming a member highly enough. There is a private Facebook group which is great for asking other members advice and sharing knowledge and experiences. I have also recently attended one of the meetups that is organised by Daniel Barnett, and it was good to meet other members (and of course Daniel) in a more social setting. It was also a good opportunity to ask any questions you wanted and being able to get advice or support as to how they would deal with whatever you ask.

- **Tracey Seymour**, HR Manager (Head of Dept), Kumon Europe & Africa Ltd

The help and advice from other HR professionals on Facebook is really valuable, and quick. All the team enjoy the audio seminars and magazines for updates on current issues.

- **Catherine Larke**, Director | myHRdept.co.uk

WWW.HRINNERCIRCLE.CO.UK

For me it's a no brainer. We have a lot of really good contributors in the HR Inner Circle and it's more than a discussion forum and invaluable source of information. When combined with the magazine, the audio seminars and events, it is a complete service especially with Daniel's legal expertise always on hand.

- **Elizabeth Ince**, Self employed HR Consultant

Just join! It is invaluable with the resources you have at hand by joining the HR Inner Circle. Especially the Facebook Group where you can get advice or a different point of view that you may not have previously considered, outside of normal working hours which is very useful. Live Q&A's too.

- **Diana Wilks**, HR Manager, Go South Coast Ltd

HR can be complex because each and every issue will have its own set of individual circumstances. Being in the HR Inner Circle enables you to bounce ideas around and make sure you are considering every angle and aspect, knowing your HR Inner Circle partners will have had a similar experience to share.

- **Pam Rogerson**, HR Director, ELAS Group

WWW.HRINNERCIRCLE.CO.UK